I0429121

Snippets of Richard Attenborough

Dave Farnham

Copyright © 2014 Dave Farnham

All rights reserved.

ISBN: 1502304031
ISBN-13: 978-1502304032

DISCLAIMER

While every effort has been made to ensure the
information in this book is correct, human error is always a
possibility and therefore the author cannot accept
responsibility for any inaccuracies.

CONTENTS

INTRODUCTION

Lord Richard Attenborough a famous and accomplished actor, producer, director and philanthropist was born on 29 August 1923 and died 24 August 2014, aged 90.

He set his sights on acting when he was young after watching Charlie Chaplin in The Gold Rush.

This was a goal he achieved spectacularly. He played his first film role in 1942 in the Noel Coward film In Which We Serve (and from which, ironically, his name and character were accidentally missed out in the credits). Following a war career in the RAF Film Unit he rapidly gained renown as one of Britain's leading actors, before becoming a highly successful director.

He directed 12 films, the most notable being Gandhi, which, with Ben Kingsley in the title role, won eight Oscars. His last film as director was Closing The Ring, made in 2007.

As both actor and director his career was notable for the large number of awards and nominations he gained.

But what marked him out as more than "just" a successful actor and director were his personal qualities. He was a tireless campaigner for social justice, for the disabled and for education as a force for good. He gave his time and support to a wide range of charities, and along with his wife, the actress Sheila Sim, funded a creative arts centre at Waterford Kamhlaba in Swaziland. This was named after their Daughter, Jane Holland, who tragically was among the victims of the 2004 tsunami.

He modestly attributed his "do-gooding" qualities to his upbringing: his parents were deeply concerned with not just talking about, but also doing what they saw as right, taking into their home and adopting two orphaned Jewish girls, escapees from Nazi Germany.

Like his parents he was a committed supporter of the Labour Party, taking the Labour bench in the House of Lords; but he was also widely admired and respected across the political spectrum for his warmth of personality and his humanity.

The quotations in this book have been selected to shed light on the man himself, his personality and his art.

RICHARD SAMUEL ATTENBOROUGH, 1925 – 2014

AN OVERVIEW OF HIS LIFE

Nickname: Dickie

29 August 1925 Born in Cambridge. Parents Frederick, Cambridge University don, (later Principal of University College Leicester) and Mary, founder member of the Marriage Guidance council. Two younger brothers; John (who died in 2012) and David.

Educated at Wyggeston Grammar School, Leicester.

1935 Saw Charlie Chaplin's film The Gold Rush, which inspired him to become an actor.

1940 Gained scholarship to Rada

1942 First film role, in Noel Coward film, In Which We Serve. Film credits accidentally omitted his name and character.

1943 Successful stage role as Pinkie Brown in Brighton Rock.

1943 Joined RAF, volunteering to fly with Film Unit to record outcomes of bombing raids.

1945 Married actress Sheila Sim. They had three children: Michael, Charlotte and Jane.

1947 Starred in John Boulting's film version of Brighton Rock.

1952 Richard and Sheila became members of original cast of Agatha Christie's The Mousetrap, in which they bought shares. The play is still running in London.

1950s – 1999 Appeared in many films, including Private's Progress (1956), I'm All Right Jack, (1959), The Great Escape (1963), Séance On A Wet Afternoon (1964), Guns At Batasi (1964),   The Sand Pebbles (1966), Doctor Doolittle (1967), 10, Rillington Place (1971), The Chess Players (1977), The Human   Factor (1979) and Jurassic Park (1993). The entry in imdb.com lists 94 appearances in films, television and video games.

1959 Formed production company Beaver Films, whose early films included The League Of Gentlemen (1960), The Angry Silence (1960) and Whistle Down The   Wind (1961). He appeared in the first two of these.

1969 - 2007 Directed twelve films, starting with Oh! What A Lovely War, a film version of Joan Littlewood's stage musical, and continuing with Young Winston (1972, the first of several biographical films), A Bridge Too Far (1977),   Magic (1978), Gandhi (1982), A Chorus Line (1987), Cry Freedom (1987), Chaplin (1992), Shadowlands

(1993), In Love And War (1996),Grey Owl (1999), Closing The Ring (2007).

1980 – 1986 Deputy Chairman, Channel 4 TV

1986 – 1992 Chairman Channel 4 TV

2004 Lost several members of his family in the Boxing Day Tsunami, including his daughter, Jane, who was holidaying in Phuket, Thailand.

2008 Suffered heart problems, resulting in hospitalisation in August and fitted with pacemaker. A fall in December resulted in further stay in hospital and several days in a coma.

2012 Entered a retirement home for elderly actors in London with his wife Sheila.

2014 Died in nursing home, lunchtime, August 24th.

Honours:

CBE, 1967
Knighted,1976
Life Peer,1993
Vice-President of British Academy of Film & Television Arts (BAFTA), 1971-94
Honorary D.Litt, University of Leicester, 1970
Honorary D.Litt, University of Kent, 1981
Honorary D.Litt, University of Sussex, 1987
Freeman of the City of Leicester, 1990
Fellow of King's College, London, 1993
Elected Chancellor of University of Sussex
President of BAFTA, 2002
President of Rada, 2003
Life President of Chelsea Football Club, 2008

Film Awards (with award dates)

Oscar:

> Best Picture: Gandhi, (1982)
> Best Director: Gandhi, (1982)

Golden Globe:

> Best Director: Gandhi (1982)
> Best Supporting Actor: Doctor Doolittle (1968)
> Best Supporting   Actor: The Sand Pebbles (1967)

BAFTA:

> Shadowlands (1994)
> Best Film: Gandhi (1983)
> Best Direction: Gandhi (1983)
> Best British Actor: Guns At Batasi (1964)
> Best British Actor: Séance On A Wet Afternoon (1964)

Berlin Film Festival:

> Honourable Mention: Cry Freedom (1987)

David di Donatello Awards:

> Best Foreign Film: Gandhi (1983)

Directors Guild of America:

> Outstanding Directorial Achievement: Gandhi (1983)

Evening Standard British Film Awards:

Best Film: A Bridge Too Far (1978)

Guild of German Art House Cinemas:

Foreign Film Gold Award: Gandhi (1985)

Heartland Film Festival:

Studio Crystal Heart Award: Shadowlands (1994)

Italian National Syndicate of Film Journalists:

IFTA Award: Best Foreign Director (1983)

San Sebastian International Film Festival:

Prize San Sebastian:Best Actor: séance On A Wet Afternoon (1964)

Zulueta Prize: Best Actor: The League Of Gentlemen (1960)

Charitable Involvements

• Chairman Muscular Dystrophy Campaign: founded the Richard Attenborough Fellowship Fund

• Active on behalf of United World Colleges

• Founded (with his wife) the Jane Holland Creative Centre for Learning at Waterford Kamhlaba, Swaziland, named after their daughter who died in the 2004 Tsunami

- Actors Charitable Trust: Chairman 1956-88, President 1988-2012

- Cinema and Television Benevolent Fund council member

- Combined Theatrical Charities Appeal council member 1964-88

- Help A London Child, founder and Patron 1998-2014

- UNICEF Goodwill Ambassador 1987-2014

- Amnesty International Patron 1997-2014

- One World Action, Patron1992-2014

ON FILMS, DIRECTING, ACTORS AND ACTING

On being a film actor in the 1950s

I was bored stiff with much of the acting I was doing. I made some dreadful films. Most of the films were to pay the gas bill.

*

I want cinema to contribute to argument, to antagonism, to anger, whatever, but always related to human affairs and human decency.

*

I found it harder growing up than Mickey Mouse. I was becoming haunted by the stigma of my simpering, whining image. Then, one day, I read a critic who said I had become the boy next door to dreariness and suddenly I knew my career was very sick indeed.

I became a producer as I really believed that was the only way I could stay in the business.

*

David (his brother) has asked me, a number of people have asked me and said, 'What performance do you like best?' or 'What's the best film you've made?' and so on and I don't really have any hesitation that the film I'm least embarrassed by and ashamed of or uneasy about is Shadowlands.

*

In an interview with the Leicester Mercury, he recalls his first production, a show at St Barnabas Hall in Leicester

It's part of my need to revolt against the early Dickie Attenborough fan image – you know, the Peter Puberty of Charm School, which I set to efface by deliberately playing middle-aged roles.

*

In the late 1940s, there weren't any pop stars and TV didn't exist. We lived in Chelsea, and it came to a point where we couldn't go shopping on the Kings Road. We brought crowds to a halt. I came to hate it.

*

He (an American critic) said something like, 'the problem with Attenborough's work is that he is more interested in the content than the execution.' Almost without exception that is true. I am glad to say I am sorry if I'm not more adventurous cinematically. But my concern is always, did the film say what I wanted to express or advocate?

*

On the advice Indian Prime Minister Pandit Nehru gave him

I spent quite a bit of time with him, and he gave me valuable advice. I suppose Nehru was closer to Gandhi than anyone else. He willingly said, 'Look, he had all the frailties, all the shortcomings. Give us that. That's the measure, the greatness of a man.' On one occasion in 1963 or '64, I don't remember which, I'd gone to say goodbye to Nehru. I didn't know it'd be the last time I'd see him. As I was leaving — looking for a taxi, I think — Nehru came down the stairs and said: 'Richard, one last thing. In your film, don't deify him. He was too great a man to be turned into a god.

*

On skepticism by producers that no one would pay to see an epic-length drama – Gandhi –with Ben Kingsley

They were all terrified of the subject matter, they thought it was totally uncommercial, they wanted a major movie name to play the lead and I was absolutely determined not to have a star in the part. At one point Paramount [Pictures] actually said they'd give me the money if Richard Burton could play Gandhi.

*

Richard Attenborough risked most of his life savings to cover the $22 million that the film 'Gandhi' cost him to make. He went to the extent of mortgaging his

house, sold possessions and even acted in films that he described as "terrible crap" to help pay for his obsession for making it. (The film eventually made back 20 times what it was expected to make)

I don't have any wish to play to a few people in an art house. When you're making a movie that's costing a fortune, whatever you want to convey had to be in the terms of a world mass media.

*

Movies have given me a part of my life where I can express feelings and bring convictions to an audience as if I could write. So I made Gandhi about human relations, prejudice and the empire. In Cry Freedom I expressed my horror and disgust about apartheid.

*

Hollywood would not finance the film 'Ganhdi'

 "Who wants to see a movie about a little brown guy dressed in a sheet, carrying a beanpole?" one studio representative said scornfully'

*

After Bafta has just held a celebration for the 25th anniversary of Gandhi.

It was marvellous. They screened it on 70mm. Quite a revelation. Though it was too long. It took me 20 years to get the money to get that movie made. I remember my pitch to 20th Century Fox. The guy said: "Dickie, it's sweet of you to come here. You're obviously obsessed. But who the f---ing hell will be interested in a little brown man wrapped in a sheet carrying a beanpole?" I would have loved to have met that guy after the Oscars and told him to f--- off.

*

After criticism for making his biopic of Gandhi

I'm upset that so many Indian filmmakers are worried. But let's get the facts straight. It has been a long time since Gandhi died and none of them has come up with a film.

*

My passion emanates from pioneering wartime documentary films like Western Approaches, Desert Victory and Fires Were Started. They were made by a group of marvellous film-makers who did so much for British cinema. Those movies, made in the middle of the war, said to us all: 'This is reality. This is the truth. This is the way ordinary sailors, soldiers and civilians speak.'

The best elements of British cinema, our best directors, have never deserted that. We're at our best when we tell our own stories. When we present who we are, there's a veracity about it. When our films really work, it's because they're indigenous, like The Full Monty, Calendar Girls, Trainspotting or Dirty Pretty Things.

*

I was brought up in the David Lean era. I haven't altered my style over the years. I haven't moved greatly forward with the impact of television editing and such. Perhaps I should have. Composition is very important to me. Time spent on a piece of composition, as it was with David Lean, is one of the things that gives me joy.

*

Fifty years ago, there were great impresarios like Jack Warner who ran the industry. They would read a script and say, "Yeah, we'll do it," and it was done and nobody else was involved. There is no such person in the industry now. I went to the head of one of the major studios and tried to persuade him to make a movie, and his reply was, "I'll give it to our marketing people, and I'll let you know". He didn't give a shit about the subject, or the film. The excitement, creativity and the importance of emotional impact goes. To deal with the studios now is absolute hell, not because they're shits, but because they're all 23 year olds and they've never been in front of a camera, they have no ideas of how you actively create cinema

*

The truth of the fact is that we used 400,000 people in that scene, and I do think it had an extraordinary impact on the screen. I don't enjoy people saying to me, "Oh you can now do it this way now". I want it to be real.

*

Of course, I'd rather have nice things written about me, but I'm not a great auteur, I'm not a great director. I'm a good director. I have an ability to make people examine certain circumstances.

*

I'm an ensemble director. I do think I can get wonderful performances out of actors.

*

I knew it was the proper thing to have an interval during a show, so I gave out that there would be one of 20 minutes. 'Nonsense,' said a voice in the audience. 'Ten minutes is quite long enough.

A lot of directors don't like actors - they think they get in the way: Powell, Lean, Hitchcock. But my confidence as a director comes from knowing that I can act.

*

Diana Hawkins (his business partner) and I went to see ET in Los Angeles shortly before all the awards and we used language when we came out, to the extent of saying 'We have no chance – ET should and will walk away with it'...

Without the initial premise of Mahatma Gandhi, the film would be nothing. Therefore it's a narrative film but it's a piece of narration rather than a piece of cinema, as such.

ET depended absolutely on the concept of cinema and I think that Steven Spielberg, who I'm very fond of, is a genius.

I think ET is a quite extraordinary piece of cinema.

*

There's nothing more important in making movies than the screenplay.

*

Forbesy (Bryan Forbes) and I were playing silly parts, and we were typecast, and we didn't feel the sort of movies that we were being asked to play in were things we wanted to play in greatly.

*

If you're not prepared or interested in science fiction, which in terms of movies I'm not, if you're not interested in terms of all the CGI stuff that you can now do in the cinema which is quite remarkable compared to the time that I was making movies, 30, 40, 50 years ago, then if you're not prepared to indulge in the pornography of violence or overt sexual matter, it's very, very difficult. It is hard to raise the money.

*

The cost of promoting movies, the advertising and promotion of a movie, the budget is almost as large as the cost of the movie.

Huge blockbusters that you see have tens and hundreds of millions of pounds and dollars spent promoting them. And if you don't have something which they believe will reach an enormous audience, then they won't go for it. And so you fall out. And there are companies in the UK, terrific companies, young companies, who made, you know, whether it be Four Weddings and a Funeral (1994) or whatever, or Trainspotting (1996) or whatever, who are having a go, but it is not any easier, in fact I think it's even probably more difficult than it was when Forbesy and I were starting, which is a pity.

*

He chose actors for films

...who I think are tremendous because I believe that we, all of us, identify with subject not intellectually easily, but we identify with human beings who we believe are real human beings, four-dimensional human beings, that I understand.

*

About directing actors

You have one operation, which is commanding a regiment, commanding an army. You either enjoy it or you don't. I do. I love organising and making all the logistics work

The scenes played by one or two people who have lines are just as important, even set against that huge panorama.(He was referring to the funereal scene in 'Gandhi').

And that is how I employ my time in cinema, saying things about people who I think have touched us in terms of our value judgement and by example.

*

I hate and despise the pornography of violence. I don't believe that we can totally excuse ourselves from that situation. I believe that both cinema and film to a certain extent have encouraged it.

*

I have a bald pate, and the make-up took something like three and a half hours each day.

*

What would tempt him back into acting

If Steven (Spielberg) asked me to do Jurassic Park 4, then I'd jump at it, but that's about it.

*

He wanted to make films until his death

On my last day of shooting, I'd be happy to say 'Cut, it's a wrap' and fall off the twig.

*

I only care about style that serves the subject.

*

Why he was never a traditional leading man but always a character actor

I'm 4ft 2ins, and not exactly a matinee idol.(He was in fact 5ft 7 ins.)

*

He compartmentalised in order to cope when acting

If you are playing in Charley's Aunt and your favourite aunt died that lunchtime, you'll still have to go on the stage and play Charley's Aunt.

You have to be able to separate things. I can't think of Ginny (his daughter Jane) all the time. I think of Ginny when my mind allows me to.

*

He wanted, but was unable to raise the funds to make a film about the American philosopher and revolutionary Thomas Paine

I think **Tom Paine** is one of the greatest men that's ever lived.

*

About Kevin Kline

A complex character, a total chameleon - and an engaging and bewitching man. He can charm the birds off the trees, but he is also terribly shy.

*

Pier Angeli was in the movie called Sea of Sand that Guy Green directed where this idea came up.

*

Love and War had a wonderful performance by Sandy, **Sandra Bullock**, who the authorities and, the supposed authorities, in cinema didn't want to know about.

*

You cannot think of cinema in the UK and not place Chaplin in the most extraordinary elevated context, if there can be such a thing, in that he was a genius, he was unique.

*

Diana Dors - life was never dull for our very own bombshell.

HIS OPINIONS ON CAPITAL
PUNISHMENT, AGING AND DEATH

I am passionately opposed to capital punishment, and I have been all my life.

*

I think it is obscene that we should believe that we are entitled to end somebody's life, no matter what that person has supposedly done or not done.

*

At my age the only problem is with remembering names. When I call everyone darling, it has damn all to do with passionately adoring them, but I know I'm safe calling them that. Although, of course, I adore them too.

*

My short-term memory is a disaster. I'm trying to write my autobiography at the moment, co-writing it with my long-term friend and collaborator Diana Hawking... she's always saying, "Dick, darling, you are a prick. Why can't you remember anything?

*

About war

I find it agonising to contemplate the First World War. It was so hideous to use men as cannon fodder. Satire seems the only way to make sense of it. The Second World War was morally different. More justifiable and I think that justifies the war films, even if they do romanticise war. I joined up because of the girls. I wanted to get out there and do something because of them. (He was referring to his stepsisters, Irene and Helga, who were Jewish refugees).

*

I can recall the war in great detail, but then have blanks after that. Poppy and I were at Rada in 1941 and the back of the building was destroyed. There was a great hoo-ha about whether we could re-open. We all helped out with cardboard and nails and hammered up the windows. I remember this figure in plus-fours appeared and said in a soft Irish voice: "It's all right children; we're going to open." It was George Bernard Shaw. I could draw him to this day, get the angle of his legs as he stood there exactly right.

*

He joined the RAF in 1943 as an air-gunner cameraman. His job was to film the bombing raids as they happened and the aftermath as the plane circled

The turbulence for me was purgatory in the Lanc. It made me air sick.

...Well, because we were at high altitude we had to wear oxygen masks so I would have to take the mask off to be sick then get it quickly back on so that I didn't pass out, all the time reloading the camera. I wasn't frightened. Because I was young and stupid, I suppose. There was a bit of ack-ack, but f---k all really because this was towards the end of the movie. Did I say movie? I meant war. End of the war.

*

His tinnitus is a legacy of his involvement in the war

It was during training as a gunner. The instructor, a Corporal Wood, Timber Wood we called him, said, "Oh bugger it, I've forgotten the ear protectors, but you'll be all right." So I did the test and was deaf for a week. It smashed the eardrum in one ear and that is why I still have to wear hearing aids. It left me with terrible tinnitus but, oddly enough, as my hearing has got worse my tinnitus level has also gone down. A small mercy.

TRADE UNIONS

I'm a passionate trade unionist. (He was true to the character he played in the 1950s film 'Angry Silence'about a young worker who stands up to the union leadership at a large engineering plant.)

*

I believe in trade unionism, and I believe in democracy, in democratic trade unionism.

I was on my own union council for twenty-odd years.

ABOUT HIS LIFE AND FAMILY

He (his father) was a generous man, but we were all apprehensive of his displeasure. Always desperate for his approval.

The preservation of the family, as well as its potential success, was very important to my father. He didn't believe that as an actor I would be able to support a wife and child.

*

Dave was the academic and I was a washout – a considerable disappointment to the Governor (his father)

*

I came from a family who believed in, the Rights of Man, who believed that in order to justify the sort of luxurious life that the majority of us have, related to the whole world, that you had to do something.

*

My parents believed in the responsibility of one human being for another and in the idea that you had little right to experience the phenomenal joys of life unless you were aware of others who could be three feet or 3,000 miles away, facing difficulties you had no understanding of. They believed in the principle of putting something back. That, for them, was what life was about. And boy, they lived their life to the full.

*

I'm not competitive with Dave (his brother). Not one iota. In fact, I think that's given me more joy than almost anything, Dave's unparalleled success.

What's terribly funny, of course, is that we're not in the slightest bit alike. I must be five inches shorter, I'm tubby, Dave's very thin. I suppose there are certain mannerisms, but what people can't cope with is the similarity of our voices

*

His parents took two Jewish girls into their home when the second World War broke out - they stayed for eight years. Attenborough's father summoned his three sons to his study and spoke to them about the two girls who were in London on their way to America at the outbreak of war. He quotes his father:

'We think we ought to adopt them. But we need your agreement. There'll be fewer holidays, fewer outings. We'll be a family of seven, instead of a family of five…'

*

That particular decision, not merely paying lip service but taking positive, responsible action to help other human beings, made a profound impression on me. It has, I suppose, affected my life and my attitudes ever since.

*

Speaking about the death of his daughter Jane who died in the South Asian Tsumani on Boxing Day 2004

I can talk to people about Jane now, although sometimes I can't get the words out. I can also see her. I can feel her touch. I can hear her coming into a room. She comes in laughing or excited or determined, but always full of commitment. That was the very essence of Jane – commitment. And music.

*

I adore my family, they are my joy. However, I am committed to my work. If on a Saturday morning when I was ostensibly going to be with the children and something arose at Rada or at Unicef or at the orphanage or whatever, I would allow the other pressures to take precedent.

*

On Taking pictures of his family

None at all. Never operated a camera in my life. Never did home movies. Michael [his son] did, but not me.

*

About his marriage

A bomb went off while me and Sheila were exchanging our wedding vows you know. It was a sort of routine.

*

She (his wife, Sheila Sim, whom he affectionately called Poppy) said if we are going to make this marriage work I will have to give up acting. She never again wanted to say goodnight to the children and go to work. It kept her sane. That's why she is such a good mother.

*

As for my relationship with Poppy, well thank God I have her. I worship her. I really worship her.' He catches his breath. 'I love her like... She is the great good fortune of my life. We have had an association of such love, such laughter, such discovery for so very, very long. We've been married 62 years. It was to have been our diamond jubilee celebration the year...(emotion prevented him from saying the year of his daughter's death).

*

On living in London

Everything is nice about living in Richmond. It hasn't really changed over the years. Except the fucking aircraft. They are dreadful. They come over about every minute.

*

Coping with grief

I understand the pain of loss. We have six grandchildren aged from nine to 22 but we used to have seven.

We have two children, Michael and Lottie, and we used to have three.

The family is the focal point of our existence. And up until Jane and Lucy's death, there were always 16 of us together for Christmas. But we haven't been able to manage that emotionally. I can't bear to see the empty spaces at the table.

Sheila and I will be spending Christmas in Scotland where we can talk about Jane and Lucy, talk about our feelings and weep.

People ask 'does it get any better?', but it doesn't. You just become more capable of dealing with it.

*

You assemble armour, an ability to compartmentalise your grief, put it in a place that you can revisit when you choose. Also you learn to place it in juxtaposition with positive memories. We had 50 happy years with Jane, and 14 with Lucy(his granddaughter who he also died in the tsunami). So you can suddenly recall joy. It is available. You just have to reach down into your memory to find it. I remember when Jinny, we called her Jinny, first visited the seaside. I remember the time we took her to see a Picasso exhibition. I may still weep, but the box of memory no longer seems empty. It is not just a terrible void.

*

31

You can't outrun your grief. You have to confront it. I saw a young woman only today who made my heart jump. She had the same long blonde hair and oval face and retroussé nose...

*

Shirley (MacLaine) is one of the few people I've been able to talk to about what happened. ... She is an icon. Poppy and I worked with her 40 years ago in a terrible film called The Bliss of Mrs Blossom. The children and grandchildren are forbidden from mentioning the title because they always laugh. It is a f---ing awful title. When we met on that film her daughter was the same age as Jane so we all got to know each other as two families. Shirley was hugely sympathetic. We talked about the grieving process as a way of understanding her character. In the film she clings to the hope that her husband might not be dead because his body wasn't found. Then the ring arrives. I felt able to talk to Shirley about what she had to assimilate by virtue of what had happened to Poppy and me.

*

How grief has brought his family closer

Oddly enough it has given us a new level of connection with Michael.

...He used to make Jinny laugh until she cried. He is outrageous and vulgar, you see. He could make Jinny collapse with laughter. He misses her certainly as much as we do. He finds it difficult, as do her children, of course. The oldest, Sam, is now 22. Alice is 19.

ABOUT HIMSELF

I'm very passionate. I cry because I care. I feel things very deeply. I'm motivated by my emotions.

*

I'm not an intellectual - I left school at 16. I work by instinct, in large measure.

*

An idiotic optimist. (He called himself0

*

How he discovered that he'd won a scholarship to the Royal Academy of Dramatic Art

I had been on ARP duty and was walking back up to the side of Victoria Park where we had a house and suddenly I saw David and John pedalling towards me like crazy to tell me I had won it.

*

I can't write, I can't paint, I don't compose.

*

I do not have a brain that I long for in dealing with matters of which I am ignorant, that don't come within my ken and a rationale, a reason, and argument and so on, and I can't do that and I'm not in that bracket at all.

*

I prefer fact to fiction.

*

I don't read a great deal of fiction, to my shame, other than the classics.

I just love biography, and I'm fascinated **by people** who have shifted our destinies or our points of view.

*

When he won the only annual scholarship to Royal Academy of Dramatic Arts, of which he later became president

I remember it well. My ma took me on a train down from Leicester and we stayed in the Strand Palace Hotel. We walked over to Goodge Street, and I made her stand on the corner so it didn't look like I was being brought along by my mother.

*

On being awarded a knighthood

It was the autumn of 1975 and I remember I went down to collect the post one morning and there were two letters. I ran upstairs to tell Sheila that I'd had a letter from Downing Street and it was to say that I had been offered an appointment as a trustee of the Tate. I couldn't think of anything more wonderful – I spent half my life in the Tate on Millbank. Sheila then said, "That's lovely darling, but you said you had two letters". So I said, "Oh yes dear, I've been given a knighthood.

ABOUT POLITICS

I still couldn't vote Tory. I just couldn't. It would make me throw up

*

Labour Party leaders

I was a Kinnock man. I liked Tony, too, but became disillusioned with him over Iraq. I'm very fond of Gordon. He's a decent man and he has been the saviour of the British film industry, with his tax breaks. But he is ill-suited to the role of Prime Minister in terms of presentation and PR. Following Tony, I mean. Perhaps I shouldn't say that.

*

On heroes of today

I passionately believe in heroes, but I think the world has changed its criteria in determining who it describes as a hero...

*

If someone does something in an entertainment/pop ambience, that person becomes someone who has an impact on the conduct and attitude of a huge number of people who peripherally come in contact with them.

*

I'm simply saying that heroes are people whose activities, whose attitudes and whose judgment you just think, wow. That's good, that's right, that's real.

*

I believe we need heroes...we need certain people who we can measure our own shortcomings by.

ABOUT MODERN LIFE

I think the world is a harder place now for young people...
In the 40s and 50s, life seemed much simpler, especially in
terms of what was acceptable and what was not acceptable.
The world is also, I think, more corrupt.

*

The horror now is that the accountants and lawyers,
particularly the accountants in the huge conglomerates, no
major company stays in one conglomerate for more than
ten minutes, and you face a new set of accountants and so
on, and all they care about is what's on the bottom line.

DAVE FARNHAM

ABOUT ART

It was something that had fascinated me from the word go. When me and Sheila got married, all we had was an oval table, four chairs, a bed and a painting by Matthew Smith.

*

...art belongs to no one. Some of us are simply its temporary, fortunate and delighted custodians.

*

My philosophy has always been that I believe that art is not an elitist gift for a few select people. Art is for everyone.

DAVE FARNHAM

WHAT OTHERS HAVE SAID ABOUT HIM

His brother – Sir David Attenborough

He spent his entire childhood in the Little Theatre in Leicester and was besotted with it.

As a consequence, my father was in despair about it.

My dear brother was failing exams.

My father, as an academic, couldn't believe a son of his was failing. Poor old Dick. Of course, he hadn't done any work because he was at the theatre the whole time.

There was a thing called school certificate, the equivalent of O-Levels, and Dick failed his.

My father was at his wits' end. What was he supposed to do with this wastrel child?

He knew it was because of the theatre and he knew the

theatre was a waste of time, so he went round to all of his academic pals and said, "What is the most difficult theatrical scholarship?" They said the Royal Academy of Dramatic Arts.

'So, on Dick's 16th or 17th birthday, he said, "Now, Richard. Your exam results are disastrous.

'I know you want to be an actor, but I'm going to make a bargain. I'm going to give you, for your 17th birthday, the quite substantial fee that has to be paid to go for the Rada scholarship.

'If you get it, I will back you. If you don't, then you've got to forget about the theatre and get down and pass your A-Levels." Dick said, "Yes father", then went out and got it.

*

Michael Parkinson described him as a: Pin-up boy of the 1950s

*

David Robinson, his biographer, wrote in an 80th birthday tribute to him:

He rises early, so you are quite likely to be summoned for a 6.30am breakfast if he has to fly to Geneva on business or drive to Wales for the day.

He has an astounding capacity to cope with a dozen problems at once, allocating the necessary period of concentration to each in turn.

He is a hands-on president or chairman of a score of institutions, including Rada and the National Film and

Television School, not to speak of his roles as Chancellor of Sussex University, trustee of the Tate Gallery and life vice-president of Chelsea Football Club.

*

Nigel Farndale, journalist

When I last met Attenborough I wrote: 'He is not religious - death doesn't worry him, he says - but he has the energy, enthusiasm and goofy joyful optimism of a born-again Christian.' Some of that has gone now. He seems more subdued. But he is still tactile and still sentimental.

*

Roald Dahl

In everything he does he manages continually in some magical manner to intensify the atmosphere of suspense and doom.

*

Ronald Bergan, journalist wrote about when he played the part of serial killer John Christie in 10 Rillington Place

The sight of a chubby, bald Attenborough wearing thick glasses rubbing a corpse and moaning with orgasmic delight is particularly disturbing.

*

William Goldman, screenwriter of A Bridge Too Far

By far the most decent human being I've met in the

picture business.

*

Judith Crist, film critic,said that he had a talent for creating

A certain physical suggestion of everydayness, a certain universal but never quite mundane quality that is uniquely his.

SOME OF THE NUMEROUS TRIBUTES TO LORD ATTENBOROUGH AFTER HIS DEATH ON 24TH AUGUST 2014

Leicester people's tribute to him

He was one hell of a lovely guy

*

Sir Roger Moore

Greatly saddened to hear the great Richard Attenborough has left us. Such a wonderful and talented man

*

David Cameron

His acting in "Brighton Rock" was brilliant, his directing of "Gandhi" was stunning - Richard Attenborough was one of the greats of cinema.

*

Waterford Kamhlaba United World College of Southern Africa pays their tribute to Lord Attenborough

Waterford students will remember Lord Attenborough as a distinguished actor, producer and Oscar-winning director, but above all they will remember him as a loyal and generous friend of the United World College movement in general and Waterford in particular.

He and his wife, Lady Attenborough, visited the school on several occasions. He enjoyed discussing football with staff members and took a real interest in the students and their activities.

Lord Attenborough strongly opposed apartheid and supported Waterford, where young people of all races studied and lived together. In April 1988 he invited the IB (International Baccalaureate) to the premiere of *Cry Freedom*. The following day he hosted a private viewing of the film for the rest of the school at the Cinelux in Mbabane and took questions from the students.

He funded scholarships for many students but, being the humble, unassuming man that he was, he never sought publicity for his generosity and insisted that the students should not make a fuss about his financial support.

Lord Attenborough was a patron of the arts at Waterford. He generously funded the construction of the Sheila and Richard Attenborough Fine Arts Centre. Together with the Paul Hamlyn Foundation, he built a Drama and Music facility, the Jane Holland Centre for Creative Learning, in memory of his daughter, his granddaughter Lucy and

Jane's mother-in-law Audrey-Jane, who died in the Asian tsunami on 26 December 2004.

We are grateful for Lord Attenborough's friendship, his inspiring example of compassion and concern for others, and the artistic legacy he has left us in his remarkable films. May he rest in peace.

*

Baroness Royall of Blaisdon, Labour's leader in the House of Lords

Very sad to learn of death of Richard Attenborough, a fine man in every way. Proud that he was a Labour peer.

*

Mia Farrow

Richard Attenborough was the kindest man I have ever had the privilege of working with. A Prince. RIP 'Pa' - and thank you

*

Ricky Gervais

RIP Richard Attenborough. One of the true greats of the silver screen.

*

Robbie Collin, film critic

Richard Attenborough was a treasure of the British film industry, but he became one partly because of his readiness to be an agitator and an unsettler when necessary. As we remember him, let's not forget it.

*

Geoffrey Macnab, film critic

His work always boasted extraordinary craftsmanship and attention to performance.

*

UNICEF

We are deeply saddened by the passing of Richard Attenborough. As a UNICEF Goodwill Ambassador he was a tireless advocate for children.

*

Sir Ben Kingsley

Richard Attenborough trusted me with the crucial and central task of bringing to life a dream it took him 20 years to bring to fruition. When he gave me the part of Gandhi it was with great grace and joy. He placed in me an absolute trust and in turn I placed an absolute trust in him and grew to love him.

*

Steven Spielberg

Dickie Attenborough was passionate about everything in his life — family, friends, country and career. He made a gift to the world with his emotional epic Gandhi, and he was the perfect ringmaster to bring the dinosaurs back to life as John Hammond in Jurassic Park. He was a dear friend, and I am standing in an endless line of those who completely adored him.

*

BAFTA

We are deeply saddened to learn of the passing of esteemed filmmaker and former BAFTA President Lord Attenborough

*

Edgar Wright

If you only know the cuddly Attenborough in Jurassic Park, see him be just terrifying in Brighton Rock & 10 Rillington Place. Amazing actor.

*

David Walliams

Richard Attenborough as Pinkie in 'Brighton Rock' from 1947. One of the greatest film performances of all time.

*

Piers Morgan

Dear dear Dickie: a true legend of the screen and a delightful man.

*

Boris Becker , Former Wimbledon tennis champion

A true legend

*

Stephen Fry

Sad to hear of Dickie Attenborough. He did so so much in so many arenas.

*

Paris Barclay, The Directors Guild of America president

Lord Richard's immense contribution to the film industry has few parallels. As a director, actor and producer, he dedicated his lifetime to the arts, entertaining us from both behind and in front of the camera. As a director he took on passion projects, many of which were biographical, highlighting individuals who lived extraordinary lives, dedicated to a particular passion – much like Richard himself. A winner of the 1982 DGA Award for Outstanding Directorial Achievement in Feature Film for the biographical Gandhi, Richard was a true master filmmaker, embodying the alchemy necessary to turn film into art. He will be greatly missed.

*

Dylan McDermott

Rest in peace Richard Attenborough. U were the best Santa ever.

*

Mara Wilson

Sir Richard Attenborough was the only Santa Claus I ever believed in. A wonderful man. Still in shock right now. May he rest in peace.

*

Elizabeth Perkins

Terribly sad. He will always be my Kris Kringle. (She is referring to when Attenborough played the department store Santa who claims to be the real Kris Kringle in a remake of "Miracle on 34th Street.")

*

Richard Attenborough was the Chelsea football club's life president.

Chelsea players decided to wear black armbands for their visit to Everton out of respect for Lord Attenborough who was a lifelong supporter as well as former director at Chelsea.

The Club's tribute to him

Chelsea Football Club is tonight deeply saddened to learn of the passing of our life president Lord Attenborough, CBE at the age of 90. He led a long and successful life and always found time for the things in life he loved most, one of which was Chelsea FC.

Renowned throughout the world for his work in cinema which honoured him with awards for acting, directing and producing, football – and Chelsea in particular – was never far from his thoughts.

He will be greatly missed, and the thoughts of everyone at Chelsea FC are with his family and friends at this sad time.

*

Former Channel 4 and BBC executive Lord Grade

Dickie was essentially a man who put much more in than he ever took out of the industry.

*

Amanda Nevill, British Film Institute chief executive

He was a man of huge warmth and integrity but always a man with a cause, I think somebody who really understood that film was such a powerful tool that could be used to influence and capture hearts and change the world.

*

Diane Abbott, MP

Very sad to hear Richard Attenborough has died - a man of the establishment who was never afraid to challenge that same establishment.

*

The Labour Party, for whom he was a peer

Lord Attenborough made an enormous contribution to our country and to the film industry both as an actor and a director. His films will be loved for generations to come. He believed passionately in social justice and the Labour

Party and was a vocal campaigner against apartheid. He will be sadly missed. Our thoughts are with his family and friends.

OTHER BOOKS BY DAVE FARNHAM

Snippets of Boris Johnson

Snippets of Nigel Farage

Snippets of Jeremy Kyle

Snippets of Joan Rivers

Snippets of Paul Gascoigne

Snippets of Billy Connolly

www.ingramcontent.com/pod-product-compliance
Lightning Source LLC
Chambersburg PA
CBHW060221290526
45789CB00003B/1356